boutique *slippers*™

Designs by Lorine Mason

HOUSE of
WHITE
BIRCHES

PUBLISHERS
SINCE 1947

Boutique Slippers

Fun in the Sun Slippers,
page 28

Did you ever create shoes for yourself using cardboard and string? Well, my sister and I managed to open a few shoe stores during our childhood. We displayed a variety of shoe styles that we had fashioned from things we found around the house.

Our design process usually involved one of us standing on a piece of cardboard while the other traced around her feet, allowing an inch or so for extra foot protection. We would carefully cut out our patterns and then discuss the next step in our shoe-design process. Would we be creating a simple flip-flop, or a more detailed style of ballet slipper? We soon expanded our design styles to include pumps and sandals, adding heels with layer upon layer of cardboard. What a hoot! I think back and wish someone had thought to take a photo; now that would have made a fun scrapbooking page.

When asked to create *Boutique Slippers*, my first thought was that I would like to use my sister Gayle's feet as my pattern. But, alas, she is back home in Manitoba so I have decided to use my own feet. Luckily, we are similar in size so I might send her a pair when I am done. They will not be quite the same as back on the farm, but I am pretty sure we will have a few laughs remembering cutting the ribbon at the grand opening of our first shoe store.

Lorine

Slippers Squared With Clips,
page 24

Table of Contents

Floral Ballet Slippers,
page 11

Slipper Booties With Clips,
page 14

Asian Flower Slippers,
page 20

*Pastel Slip-ons
With Clips, **page22***

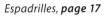

*Espadrilles, **page 17***

House of White Birches, Berne, Indiana 46711 Clotilde.com

The Basics

Fat Quarters
A fat quarter is a half yard of fabric cut in half along the fold, giving the buyer approximately 18 x 22 inches of fabric.

Stiff Fusible Interfacing
Choose a heavy-weight fusible craft interfacing. It is usually recommended for use in creating anything requiring a great deal of body such as a purse, costumes or slippers. It can be found at local fabric stores, where it is available by the yard as well as in precut packages.

Cotton Batting
Use 100 percent cotton batting for the slippers. It is available in precut packages as well as by the yard at your local fabric store.

Nonslip Fabric/Faux Leather
When looking for items to add strength and wear-ability to the soles of your slippers, check what is available at your local fabric store. Both nonslip fabrics and faux leathers work well. Both can be found in local fabric stores and are available by the yard, by the piece and in precut packages.

Clip-on Earring Blanks
Clip-on earring blanks can be found in the jewelry section of craft and hobby stores. Glue decorations such as buttons, yo-yos, bows and jewelry to the flat side of a blank earring clip using an all-purpose permanent adhesive.

Embellishments
There are a variety of embellishments such as ribbon, buttons, silk flowers or self-adhesive flat-backed pearls. The choice really is yours; decide by color, texture or theme. Attach items that are not washable to removable earring clips so that they can be removed before throwing your slippers into the washing machine.

Helpful Techniques

Making Bias Binding

1. To cut bias strips, fold fabric diagonally so crosswise grain straight edge is parallel to selvage or lengthwise grain. Cut fabric along this fold line to mark the true bias (Figure 1).

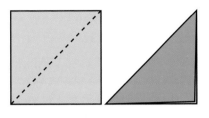

Figure 1

2. Using a clear ruler, mark successive bias lines the width of the bias strip desired. Carefully cut along line. Handle edges carefully to avoid stretching (Figure 2).

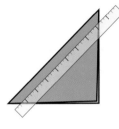

Figure 2

3. Pin individual bias strips perpendicular to each other with raw edges aligned and right sides together. Sew a diagonal seam to join strips in a continuous strip. Trim seams to ¼ inch and press open (Figure 3).

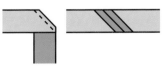

Figure 3

4. Fold strip in half lengthwise, wrong sides together. Press. Open with wrong side up. Fold each edge to center fold and press. Fold in half again and press (Figure 4).

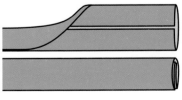

Figure 4

Blanket Stitch

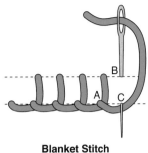

Blanket Stitch

Thread Loop

Stitch a ½-inch-wide thread loop to the front of each slipper so that an earring clip embellishment can easily be slid on and off. Create the thread loop by using an embroidery needle and pearl cotton. Tie a knot at the end of the thread and stitch back and forth through all layers of the slipper front three or four times, creating a thread loop.

Sizing

Patterns are provided in small, medium and large sizes.

Small (S) – approximately woman's shoe size 5/6

Medium (M) – approximately woman's shoe size 8/9

Large (L) – approximately woman's shoe size 9/10

The espadrilles are given only in large size.

These are only guidelines. Please take the time to test the size before starting your project. Adjust the length by cutting off or adding to the pattern. The distance between the heel and toe sections will vary depending on the adjustment to the length of the sole.

Adjust the elastic length as well, depending on the size of wearer, pulling it tighter and trimming away excess if needed. ❖

Mary Jane Slippers
& Travel Bag

Slipper

Materials
- Coordinating fat quarters:
  - 1 polka dot
  - 1 floral
  - 1 stripe
- 11 x 15 inches faux leather
- 15 x 22 inches cotton batting
- 10 x 14 inches stiff fusible interfacing
- 28 inches ¼-inch-wide elastic
- 14 inches ½-inch-wide elastic
- 2 (½-inch) buttons
- Yo-yo makers for medium and large yo-yos
- Nonstick pressing sheet
- Basic sewing supplies and equipment

Cutting
Use pattern templates A, B and C on pages 32, 33 and 34. Transfer pattern markings to fabric pieces.

From polka-dot fat quarter:
- Cut two slipper tops (C) on fold.

From floral fat quarter:
- Cut two slipper tops (C) on fold for lining.

From stripe fat quarter:
- Cut two soles (A), reversing one.
- Cut two 2 x 10-inch strips for band.

From faux leather:
- Cut two soles (A), reversing one.

From batting:
- Cut two slipper tops (C) on fold.

From stiff fusible interfacing:
- Cut two interfacing soles (B), reversing one.

Assembly
Instructions are given to create one slipper. Repeat the instructions to create a second slipper. Use a ½-inch seam allowance unless otherwise specified.

1. Pin batting slipper top to the wrong side of polka-dot slipper top and baste around the outside edge using a ¼-inch seam (Figure 1).

Figure 1

2. With right sides together, stitch the center back seam. Press seam open.

3. Stitch the center back seam of the floral slipper top lining, right sides together. Press seam open.

4. With right sides together, pin slipper top and lining sections together along the upper edges and stitch (Figure 2).

Figure 2

5. Turn right side out so that the batting is between the fabric layers and press. Topstitch ⅜-inch from the seam to make casing for elastic, leaving a 1-inch opening along one side (Figure 3).

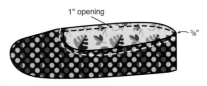

Figure 3

6. Topstitch two additional rows of stitching ¼-inch apart and ¼-inch below the elastic casing stitching (Figure 4).

Figure 4

7. Thread a 14-inch length of ¼-inch-wide elastic through casing. Overlap the ends and stitch to secure. Allow the elastic to slide back into the casing and stitch the opening closed.

8. With right sides together, fold the 2 x 10-inch stripe band in half lengthwise and stitch using a ¼-inch seam. Turn right side out, center seam along back and press flat.

9. Thread a 7-inch length of ½-inch elastic through stripe band. Pin ends of elastic even with ends of band and stitch to secure (Figure 5).

Figure 5

10. Pin band to slipper top at positions marked on the outside edge of template (C). Baste in place.

11. Pin slipper top to right side of stripe fabric sole, matching center fronts and center backs. Stitch seam, clipping seam as needed around the curves (Figure 6).

Figure 6

12. Press seam to the wrong side of sole and topstitch ¼ inch from seam to hold in place (Figure 7).

Figure 7

13. Center the interfacing sole (B) on the wrong side of the faux leather sole (A) and press using a nonstick pressing sheet (Figure 8).

Figure 8

14. Clip the curves of the faux leather edges and press the faux leather over the interfacing edges.

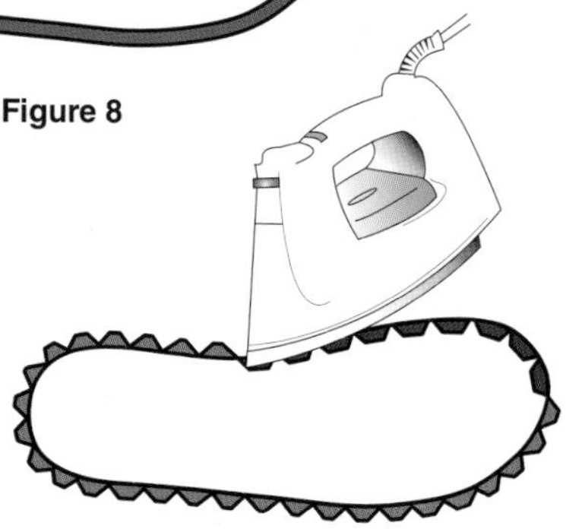

Figure 9

15. With wrong sides together, pin the faux leather sole to the stripe fabric sole sewn to the slipper top in step 11.

16. Sew the faux leather sole to the striped fabric sole using a slip stitch (Figure 10).

Figure 10

17. Attach center of stripe band to the top of the slipper front by stitching through all layers of fabric.

18. Following the manufacturer's directions, create 2 large yo-yos from leftover polka-dot fabric and 2 medium yo-yos from leftover floral fabric. Sew one of each size yo-yo and a button to the top of the slipper to finish.

Travel Bag

Materials

- Coordinating fat quarters:
  - 1 floral
  - 1 stripe
- Polka-dot scrap
- 1¼ yards ½-inch-wide grosgrain ribbon
- 1 (½-inch) button
- Yo-yo makers for medium and large yo-yos
- Basic sewing supplies and equipment

Cutting

From floral fat quarter:
- Cut one 18 x 6-inch rectangle.

From stripe fat quarter:
- Cut one 18 x 6-inch rectangle for lining.

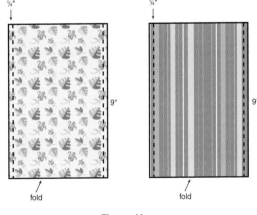

Assembly

1. With right sides together, fold each of the fabric rectangles in half. Stitch along the 9-inch length of each using a ¼-inch seam, forming two pockets (Figure 11).

Figure 11

2. Turn floral pocket right side out. Turn in top edge ½ inch and press. Turn under an additional ½ inch and press.

3. Trim ½ inch from the top edge of stripe pocket.

4. Insert stripe pocket into floral pocket wrong sides together. Tuck top raw edge of stripe pocket under the top fold of floral pocket. Edgestitch along fold (Figure 12).

Figure 12

5. Fold ribbon in half and sew to the front of the bag 2 inches below the top edge, leaving a 1½-inch loop. Join the ribbon ends together using an overhand knot. Trim ribbon ends at an angle.

6. Create 1 large floral yo-yo and 1 medium polka-dot yo-yo following the manufacturer's instructions. Sew yo-yos and button on top of the ribbon.

Note: To close bag with slippers inside, fold over top of bag, wrap ribbon around the back and up through the ribbon loop. Voilà! The ribbon tie becomes a handle. ❖

Floral Ballet Slippers

Materials

- Coordinating fat quarters:
  - 1 floral
  - 2 diamond print
- 11 x 15 inches nonslip fabric
- 15 x 22 inches cotton batting
- 10 x 14 inches stiff fusible interfacing
- 16 inches ¼-inch-wide elastic
- 2 silk flowers
- Flat-back mini pearls
- Fabric glue
- Nonstick pressing sheet
- Basic sewing supplies and equipment

Cutting

Use pattern templates A, B and C on pages 32, 33 and 34. Transfer pattern markings to fabric pieces.

From floral fat quarter:
- Cut two slipper tops (C) on fold.

From diamond print fat quarters:
- Cut two slipper tops (C) on fold for lining.
- Cut two soles (A), reversing one.

From nonslip fabric:
- Cut two soles (A), reversing one.

From batting:
- Cut two slipper tops (C) on fold.

From stiff fusible interfacing:
- Cut two interfacing soles (B), reversing one.

Assembly

Instructions are given to create one slipper. Repeat the instructions to create a second slipper. Use a ½-inch seam allowance unless otherwise specified.

1. Pin batting slipper top to the wrong side of floral slipper top and baste around the outside edge using a ¼-inch seam (Figure 1). With right sides together, stitch the center back seam. Press seam open.

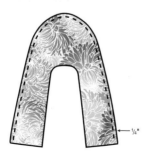

Figure 1

2. Stitch the center back seam of the diamond print slipper top lining right sides together. Press seam open.

3. Pin slipper top and lining sections right sides together along the upper edges and stitch (Figure 2).

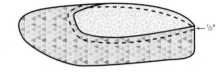

Figure 2

4. Turn right side out so that the batting is between the fabric layers and press. Topstitch ⅜ inch from the seam to make heel casing for elastic using the marking on template C as a guide (Figure 3).

Figure 3

5. Thread an 8-inch length of elastic through heel casing. Pin ends of elastic to end marks and stitch across ends to secure.

6. Pin slipper top to right side of diamond print sole, matching center fronts and center backs. Stitch seam, clipping seam as needed to achieve a smooth transition around the curves (Figure 4).

Figure 4

7. Press seam to the wrong side of sole and topstitch ¼ inch from seam to hold in place (Figure 5).

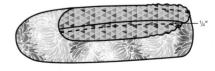

Figure 5

8. Center the interfacing sole (B) on the wrong side of the nonslip fabric sole (A) and press using a nonstick pressing sheet (Figure 6).

Figure 6

9. Clip the curves of the nonslip fabric sole edges and press the nonslip edges over the interfacing edges (Figure 7).

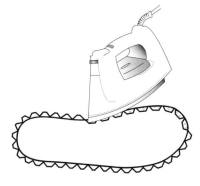

Figure 7

10. With wrong sides together, pin the nonstick fabric sole to the diamond print sole sewn to the slipper top in steps 6 and 7.

11. Sew the nonslip sole to the diamond print sole using a slipstitch (Figure 8).

Figure 8

12. Cut apart silk flowers, removing the stems and any hard plastic centers from the flowers. Hand-stitch the flower to the front of the slipper.

13. Following the fabric glue manufacturer's instructions, glue flat-back mini pearls to the slipper toe. ❖

House of White Birches, Berne, Indiana 46711 Clotilde.com

Slipper Bootie With Clips

Materials

- Coordinating fat quarters:
  - 2 green/brown print
  - 2 green batik
- 11 x 15 inches nonslip fabric
- 36 x 44 inches cotton batting
- 10 x 14 inches stiff fusible interfacing
- 8 x 11 inches fusible web
- Scraps of green and brown felt
- 2 (½-inch) brown buttons
- 2 clip-on earring blanks
- All-purpose permanent adhesive
- Pearl cotton
- Nonstick pressing sheet
- Basic sewing supplies and equipment

Cutting

Use pattern templates A, B and D on pages 32, 33, 35 and 36. Transfer markings to fabric pieces.

From green/brown print fat quarters:
- Cut four bootie tops (D), reversing two.

From green batik fat quarters:
- Cut four bootie tops (D), reversing two, for lining.
- Cut two soles (A), reversing one, for lining.

From nonslip fabric:
- Cut two soles (A), reversing one.

From batting:
- Cut four bootie tops (D).
- Cut two soles (A).

From stiff fusible interfacing:
- Cut two interfacing soles (B), reversing one.

Assembly

Instructions are given to create one slipper. Repeat the instructions to create a second slipper. Use a ½-inch seam allowance unless otherwise specified.

1. Pin batting bootie tops to the wrong side of print bootie tops and baste around the outside edge using a ¼-inch seam.

2. With right sides together, stitch the center front seam as marked on template D and center back seam (Figure 1). Press seams open.

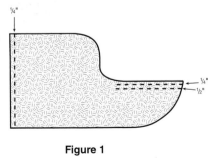

Figure 1

3. Stitch the center back and center front seams of the green batik bootie tops for lining with right sides together. Press seams open.

4. Pin bootie top and lining sections right sides together along the upper edges and stitch (Figure 2).

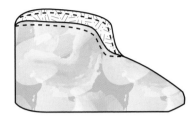

Figure 2

5. Turn right side out and press. Baste all layers together along the bottom edge using a ⅜-inch seam (Figure 3).

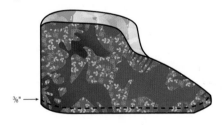

Figure 3

6. Pin sole batting to the wrong side of the green batik sole. Baste together using a ⅜-inch seam.

7. Pin bootie top to right side of green batik sole, matching center fronts and center backs. Stitch seam, clipping seam as needed around the curves (Figure 4). Press seam to the wrong side of sole.

Figure 4

8. Center the interfacing sole (B) on the wrong side of the nonslip fabric sole (A) and press using a nonstick pressing sheet (Figure 5).

Figure 5

9. Clip the curves of the nonslip fabric edges and press the nonslip fabric over the interfacing edges (Figure 6).

Figure 6

10. With wrong sides together, pin the nonslip fabric sole to the bottom of the bootie body.

11. Sew the nonslip fabric sole to the slipper using a slipstitch (Figure 7).

Figure 7

12. Create flower embellishments by fusing two layers of leftover fabric together with fusible web. Cut out flowers from fused fabric and felt using provided patterns on page 43. Stack various sizes of flowers together as desired and sew together, adding button for center.

13. Glue flower embellishment onto clip-on earring blank.

14. Use pearl cotton to stitch a thread loop to the slipper front (see page 5). Slide flower in place on slipper center front. ❖

Try dressing up the slippers by replacing the fabric flowers with a beautiful set of pearl clips.

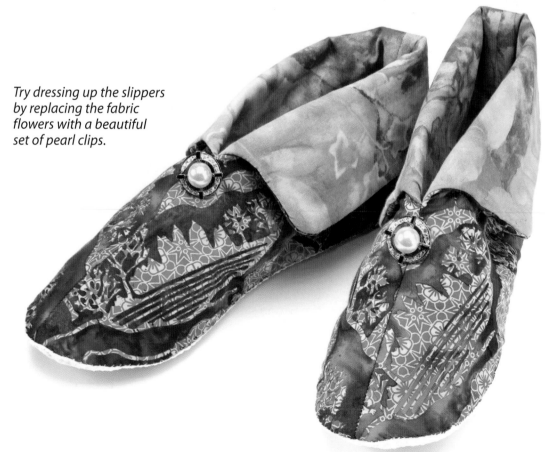

Espadrilles

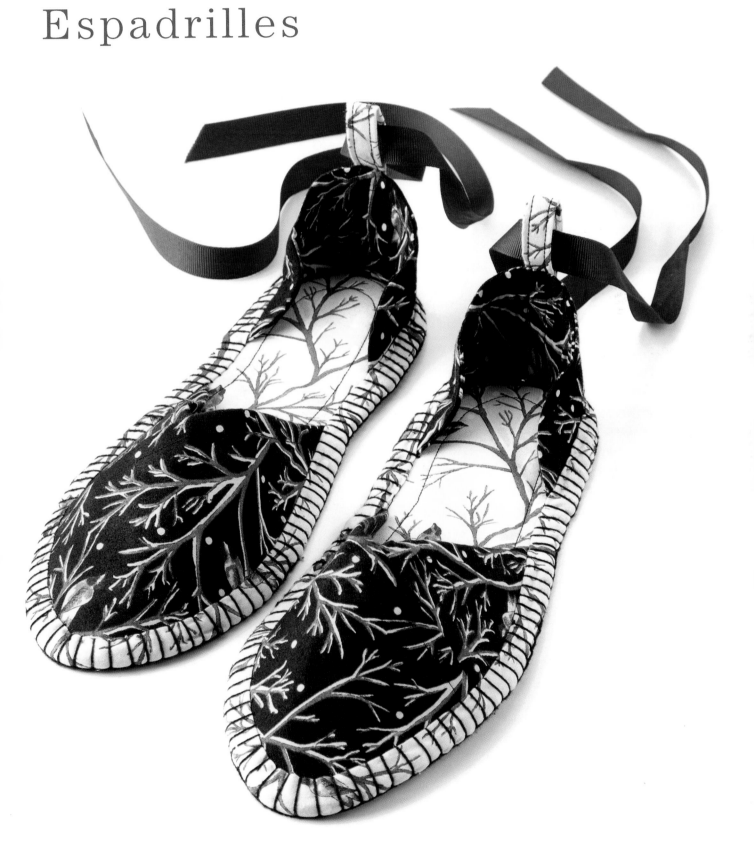

Materials
- Coordinating fat quarters:
  - 2 black print
  - 1 cream print
- 18 x 30 inches stiff fusible interfacing
- 2 yards ¾-inch-wide grosgrain ribbon
- Black pearl cotton
- Basic sewing supplies and equipment

Cutting
Use pattern templates N, O and P on pages 46 and 47. Transfer pattern markings to fabric pieces.

From black print fat quarters:
- Cut four fronts (O) on fold.
- Cut four heels (P).
- Cut two soles (N), reversing one.

From cream print fat quarter:
- Cut two soles (N), reversing one.
- Cut and prepare 72 inches of 2-inch-wide bias binding. See Making Bias Binding on page 5.

From stiff fusible interfacing*:
- Cut four fronts (O) on fold.
- Cut two heels (P).
- Cut two soles (N), reversing one.

*Note: Eliminate the seam allowances on the heel and front sections.

Assembly
Instructions are given to create one slipper. Repeat the instructions to create a second slipper. Use a ½-inch seam allowance unless otherwise specified.

1. Fold two front sections in half along fold line, wrong sides together. Insert the front interfacing pieces between folded fabric and press well, fusing the interfacing in place.

2. Topstitch ⅜ inch from the folded edge of each section. Finish the raw edges using an overcast or machine zigzag stitch (Figure 1).

Figure 1

3. With right sides together, stitch the upper edge of the heel sections together. Turn right side out and press. Insert interfacing between fabric layers and press again.

4. Topstitch ⅜ inch from the top seam and finish the raw edges with an overcast or machine zigzag stitch (Figure 2).

Figure 2

5. Cut an 8-inch piece bias binding. Topstitch ⅛ inch from either side of the binding strip. Fold the binding strip in half, forming a loop.

6. Position the loop over the center back of heel section, extending the loop 1½ inches above top of heel seam. Topstitch through all thicknesses along the top edge of the heel as well as down each side of the bias strip (Figure 3).

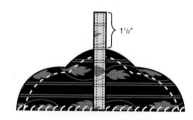

Figure 3

7. Sandwich the interfacing sole between the black print and cream print soles. Press to fuse the interfacing to the fabric. Topstitch ¾ inch all around the outside edge. Finish the raw edges with an overcast or machine zigzag stitch (Figure 4).

Figure 4

8. Pin the heel to the sole, matching the center back markings. Stitch in place using an overcast or machine zigzag stitch.

9. Pin the two front sections together, overlapping at overlap line. Pin front sections to the sole and stitch together using an overcast or machine zigzag stitch (Figure 5).

Figure 5

10. Pin bias binding over the seam along the sole edge (Figure 6).

11. Using pearl cotton, hand-stitch over the bias binding using a blanket stitch (see page 5).

12. Cut 1-yard piece of ribbon and thread through the loop on the back of espadrille. ❖

Figure 6

Asian Flower Slippers

Materials
- Coordinating fat quarters:
  2 large floral
  1 print
- 11 x 15 inches nonslip fabric
- 10 x 14 inches stiff fusible interfacing
- 16 inches ¼-inch-wide elastic
- 6 (¾-inch) buttons
- Basic sewing supplies and equipment

Cutting
Use pattern templates A, B, E, F and G on pages 32, 33, 37, 38 and 39. Transfer pattern markings to fabric pieces.

From large floral fat quarters:
- Cut four slipper tops (E), reversing two.
- Cut two soles (A), reversing one.

From print fat quarter:
- Cut two lining slipper tops (F) on fold.
- Cut two gussets (G).

From nonslip fabric:
- Cut two soles (A), reversing one.

From stiff fusible interfacing:
- Cut two interfacing soles (B), reversing one.

Assembly
Instructions are given to create one slipper. Repeat the instructions to create a second slipper. Use a ½-inch seam allowance unless otherwise specified.

1. Using ¼-inch seam and right sides together, stitch the gusset to the floral slipper top pieces, matching the seam lines.

2. Fold and press the gusset along the fold lines, creating a center pleat. Pin or baste to hold (Figure 1).

3. With right sides together, stitch the center back seam of the floral slipper top. Press seam open.

4. With right sides together, stitch the center back seam of the print slipper top lining and press seam open.

5. With right sides together, pin slipper top and lining sections together along the upper edges and stitch using a ⅜-inch seam (Figure 2). Turn lining to inside and press.

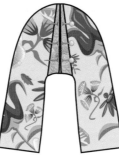

Figure 1

⟵ ⅜"

Figure 2

6. Topstitch ⅜ inch from the top edge of the slipper heel as marked on template E to make elastic casing (Figure 3).

Figure 3

7. Thread an 8-inch length of ¼-inch-wide elastic through casing. Pin ends of elastic to end marks and stitch across ends to secure.

8. Pin slipper top to the right side of print sole, matching center fronts and center backs. Stitch seam, clipping seam as needed around the curves (Figure 4).

Figure 4

9. Press seam to the wrong side of sole and topstitch ¼ inch from seam to hold in place (Figure 5).

Figure 5

10. Center the interfacing sole (B) on the wrong side of the nonslip fabric sole (A) and press using a nonstick pressing sheet (Figure 6).

Figure 6

11. Clip the curves of the nonslip fabric edges and press the nonslip fabric over the interfacing edges (Figure 7).

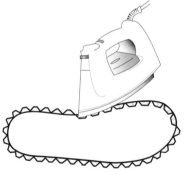

Figure 7

12. With wrong sides together, pin the nonstick fabric sole to the print sole sewn to the slipper top in step 8.

13. Sew the nonslip fabric sole to the print sole using a slipstitch (Figure 8).

Figure 8

14. Stitch three buttons evenly spaced to the front of the slipper centered over the gusset folds. ❖

House of White Birches, Berne, Indiana 46711   Clotilde.com

Pastel Slip-ons With Clips

Materials
- Coordinating fat quarters:
  - 1 large floral
  - 1 peach/white print
  - 1 light peach print
- 18 x 22 inches cotton batting
- 11 x 15 inches stiff fusible interfacing
- 2 (¾-inch) peach buttons
- 2 (½-inch) yellow buttons
- 2 clip-on earring blanks
- Air- or water-soluble marking pen
- Pearl cotton
- Basic sewing supplies and equipment

Cutting & Quilting
Use pattern templates A, M and flower circles on pages 32, 35 and 45. Transfer pattern markings to fabric pieces.

1. Using an air- or water-soluble marking pen, position and trace two slipper soles (A), reversing one, two slip-on toes (M) and two each of the circle flowers onto the right side of the large floral fat quarter (Figure 1).

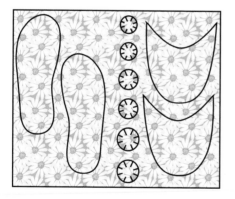

Figure 1

2. Cut the fat quarter into two sections; soles and toes/flowers referring to Figure 2.

3. Layer the soles section in the following order: peach/white fabric right side down, interfacing, batting and large floral fabric with traced soles right side up. Trim layers to match large floral section.

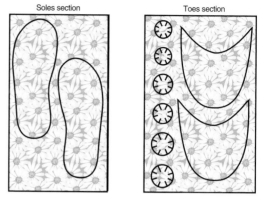

Figure 2

4. Layer the toes/flower section in the following order: peach/white fabric right side down, batting and large floral fabric with traced toes and flowers right side up. Trim layers to match large floral section.

5. Sew horizontal and vertical lines ½ inch apart through all layers of both sections (Figure 3).

6. Cut out each of the pattern pieces on traced lines.

7. From light peach fat quarter, cut and prepare 80 inches of 2-inch-wide bias binding strips, referring to Making Bias Binding on page 5.

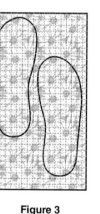

Figure 3

Assembly
Instructions are given to create one slipper. Repeat the instructions to create a second slipper. Use a ½-inch seam allowance unless otherwise specified.

1. Cut a 10-inch piece of bias binding. Open bias binding and pin to the large floral side of inner edge of the slip-on toe. Stitch along the fold line. Fold binding toward the peach/white print and topstitch through all layers (Figure 4).

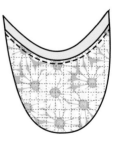

Figure 4

2. Pin slip-on toe to large floral side of sole, matching center front markings. Stitch ⅜-inch seam, clipping seam as needed around the curves (Figure 5).

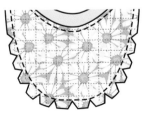

Figure 5

3. Open bias binding and position over the seam along the sole edge, right sides together, trimming excess and overlapping raw edges. Stitch bias tape in place.

4. Turn bias binding toward the bottom of the sole and hand-stitch in place (Figure 6).

5. Layer the three quilted flowers and stitch together, adding two stacked buttons. Glue to the top of a clip-on earring blank.

6. Use pearl cotton to create a thread loop on slip-on toe (see page 5). Slide clip-on flower in place. ❖

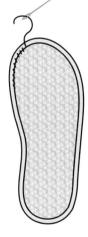

Figure 6

House of White Birches, Berne, Indiana 46711   Clotilde.com

Slippers Squared With Clips

Materials
- Coordinating fat quarters:
    - 1 aqua print
    - 1 brown/white print
    - 1 orange print
- 11 x 15 inches faux leather
- 10 x 14 inches stiff fusible interfacing
- 11 x 15 inches cotton batting
- 28 inches ¼-inch-wide elastic
- Pearl cotton
- 2 (1¼-inch) buttons*
- 2 floral charms*
- 2 clip-on earring blanks
- All-purpose permanent adhesive
- Nonstick pressing sheet
- Basic sewing supplies and equipment

Note: These items are for the fabric-covered buttons.

Cutting
Use pattern templates H, I and J on pages 40, 41 and 42. Transfer pattern markings to fabric pieces.

From aqua print fat quarter:
- Cut four slipper tops (J), reversing two.

From brown/white print fat quarter:
- Cut four slipper tops (J), reversing two, for lining.
- Cut two 1½ x 8-inch strips.

From orange print fat quarter:
- Cut two soles (H), reversing one.

From faux leather:
- Cut two soles (H), reversing one.

From batting:
- Cut two (H).

From fusible interfacing:
- Cut two interfacing soles (I), reversing one.

Assembly
Instructions are given to create one slipper. Repeat the instructions to create a second slipper. Use a ½-inch seam allowance unless otherwise specified.

1. With right sides together, stitch the center front and center back seams of the aqua print slipper top using ¼-inch seam. Press seams open.

2. Stitch the center back and center front seams of the brown/white slipper top lining right sides together using ¼-inch seam. Press seams open.

3. Pin and stitch slipper top and lining sections right sides together along the upper edges (Figure 1).

Figure 1

4. Turn right side out and press. Topstitch ⅜ inch from the seam to make casing for elastic, leaving a 1-inch opening along one side (Figure 2).

Figure 2

5. Thread a 14-inch length of elastic through casing. Overlap the ends and stitch to secure. Allow the elastic to slide back into the casing and stitch the opening closed.

6. Fold the 1½ x 8-inch brown/white strip in half lengthwise, wrong sides together and press. Open flat and fold each long edge to center and press (Figure 3a). Topstitch ⅛-inch from the folded edges (Figure 3b).

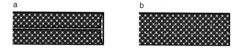

Figure 3

7. Fold the band in half widthwise, forming a loop. Center the loop over the back seam of slipper with the loop extending ½ inch above the top edge of the slipper. Topstitch along the top edge of the heel and close to each edge of band through all layers referring to Figure 4.

Figure 4

8. Pin sole batting to the wrong side of the orange print sole. Baste together using a ⅜-inch seam.

9. Pin slipper top to orange fabric sole, matching center fronts and center backs. Stitch ⅜-inch seam, clipping seam as needed around the curves (Figure 5). Remove basting.

Figure 5

10. Press seam to the wrong side of sole and topstitch ¼ inch from seam to hold in place (Figure 6).

Figure 6

11. Center the interfacing sole (I) on the wrong side of the faux leather sole (H) and press using a non-stick pressing sheet (Figure 7).

Figure 7

12. Clip the curves of the faux leather edges and press the faux leather over the interfacing edges.

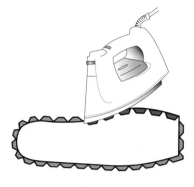

Figure 8

13. With wrong sides together, pin the faux leather sole to the orange fabric sole, sewn to the slipper in step 9.

14. Sew the faux leather sole to the orange fabric sole using a slipstitch (Figure 9).

Figure 9

15. Use pearl cotton to stitch a thread loop centered on the slipper front (see page 5). Slide clip-on embellishment in place.

Fabric-Covered Buttons

1. Lay buttons onto the wrong side of leftover brown/white fabric and trace. Add a generous ½-inch seam allowance all around each one. Cut out both circles.

2. Hand-stitch a running stitch around the outside edge of one circle. With button centered on the circle, pull the thread to gather the fabric around the button, stitching to secure in place. Repeat for second button.

3. Glue a small floral charm to the front of each covered button. Glue each covered button to the back of a clip-on earring blank.

Fabric Bows

1. Cut two bows (K, page 43) from leftover aqua fabric and two bows (K) from brown/white print fabric. Use one of each fabric for each bow.

2. With right sides together, stitch around the outside edge, leaving a 2-inch opening along one side. Turn right side out, slipstitch opening closed and press.

3. Cut two 1 x 3-inch aqua fabric strips. Turn under the long raw edges ¼" and press, creating a ½ x 3-inch band.

4. Gather each bow at the center points, forming pleats (Figure 10).

Figure 10

5. Fold each bow in half and wrap one of the bands around the pleats approximately ½ inch down from the fold (Figure 11). Hand-stitch the band to the bow. Trim away excess fabric from the band.

6. Glue bows to clip-on earring blanks. ❖

Figure 11

House of White Birches, Berne, Indiana 46711   Clotilde.com

Fun in the Sun Slippers

Materials

- Coordinating fat quarters:
    2 prints
    2 stripes
- 18 x 30 inches cotton batting
- 10 x 14 inches stiff fusible interfacing
- 28 inches ¼-inch-wide elastic
- 2 (1-inch) buttons
- Nonstick pressing sheet
- Basic sewing supplies and equipment

Cutting

Use pattern templates A, B and L on pages 32, 33 and 44. Transfer pattern markings to fabric pieces.

From print fat quarters:
- Cut two slipper tops (L) on fold.
- Cut four fabric soles (A), reversing two.

Note: One pair of soles will be for the inner soles and the other pair for the outer soles.

From stripe fat quarters:
- Cut two slipper tops (L) on fold.
- Cut three 3 x 22-inch strips.
- Cut and prepare 20 inches of 2-inch-wide bias binding. See Making Bias Binding on page 5.

From batting:
- Cut two slipper tops (L) on fold.
- Cut two fabrics soles (A).

From stiff fusible interfacing:
- Cut two interfacing soles (B), reversing one.

Assembly

Instructions are given to create one slipper. Repeat the instructions to create a second slipper. Use a ½-inch seam allowance unless otherwise specified.

Slipper Body

1. Cut a 6-inch length of bias binding. Open up last fold and center bias strip down the center front of the slipper top. Topstitch ⅛ inch from each folded edge (Figure 1).

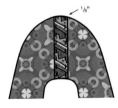

Figure 1

2. Pin and baste batting slipper top to the wrong side of print slipper top around the outside edge using a ¼-inch seam (Figure 2).

3. With right sides together, stitch the center back seam. Press seam open.

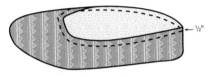

Figure 2

4. Stitch the center back seam of the stripe slipper top lining right sides together. Press seam open.

5. With right sides together, pin and stitch slipper top and lining sections together along the upper edges, referring to Figure 3.

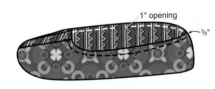

Figure 3

6. Turn right side out and press. Topstitch ⅜ inch from the seam to make casing for elastic, leaving a 1-inch opening along one side (Figure 4).

1" opening

⅜"

Figure 4

7. Thread a 14-inch length of elastic through casing. Overlap the ends and stitch to secure. Allow the elastic to slide back into the casing and stitch the opening closed.

8. Cut a 3-inch length of bias binding. Open up last fold and center it over the back seam of the slipper, turning under the top edge even with slipper edge. Stitch along both folded edges of the bias strip, covering the seam (Figure 5).

Figure 5

Pleated Ruffle

1. Join the three 3 x 22-inch stripe fabric strips together using ¼-inch seams. Press seams open.

2. Fold the pieced strip right sides together in half lengthwise and sew along the raw edges, forming a tube.

3. Turn right side out and press, centering the seam (Figure 6). Cut the sewn strip in half. Lay one half aside for use on second slipper.

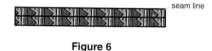

Figure 6

4. Turn raw edges ¼ inch to inside at the beginning of the strip and press.

5. Align the edge of the fabric strip along a measuring tape anchored to a table. Use a fabric marker to mark 1-inch increments on the strip (Figure 7).

Figure 7

6. Starting from the left end of the strip, skip the first mark and then fold the second mark to the third mark and pin. Fold the fourth mark to the fifth, continuing until you reach the end of the strip (Figure 8). Hand or machine-baste at top of pleats. Press and remove pins.

Figure 8

7. Beginning at the center back with the folded end, pin the pleated ruffle to the slipper just below the casing stitching. Trim any excess from the end of the pleated strip, leaving just enough to insert into the folded edge at the beginning. Topstitch in place (Figure 9).

Figure 9

Completing the Slipper

1. Pin batting sole to the wrong side of one print fabric sole to make the inner sole and baste around outside edge using ¼-inch seam.

2. Pin slipper top to right side of inner sole with batting, matching center fronts and center backs. Stitch seam, clipping seam as needed around the curves (Figure 10).

Figure 10

3. Press seam to the wrong side of inner sole and topstitch ¼ inch from seam to hold in place (Figure 11).

Figure 11

4. Center the interfacing sole on the wrong side of the second print sole and press using a nonstick pressing sheet (Figure 12).

Figure 12

5. Clip the curves of the print sole edges and press the print over the interfacing edges to make the outer sole (Figure 13).

Figure 13

6. With wrong sides together, pin the outer sole to the inner sole sewn to the slipper top in step 2.

7. Sew the outer sole to the slipper using a slipstitch (Figure 14).

Figure 14

8. Sew a button to the center top of slipper. ❖

House of White Birches, Berne, Indiana 46711   Clotilde.com

Pattern Templates

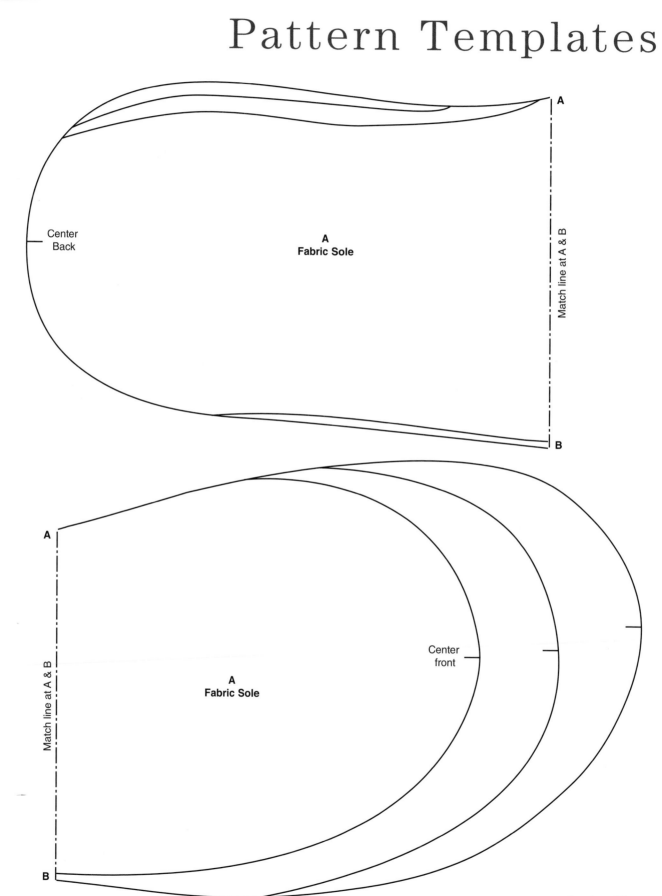

A
Fabric Sole

Center
Back

A

Match line at A & B

B

A

Match line at A & B

A
Fabric Sole

Center
front

B

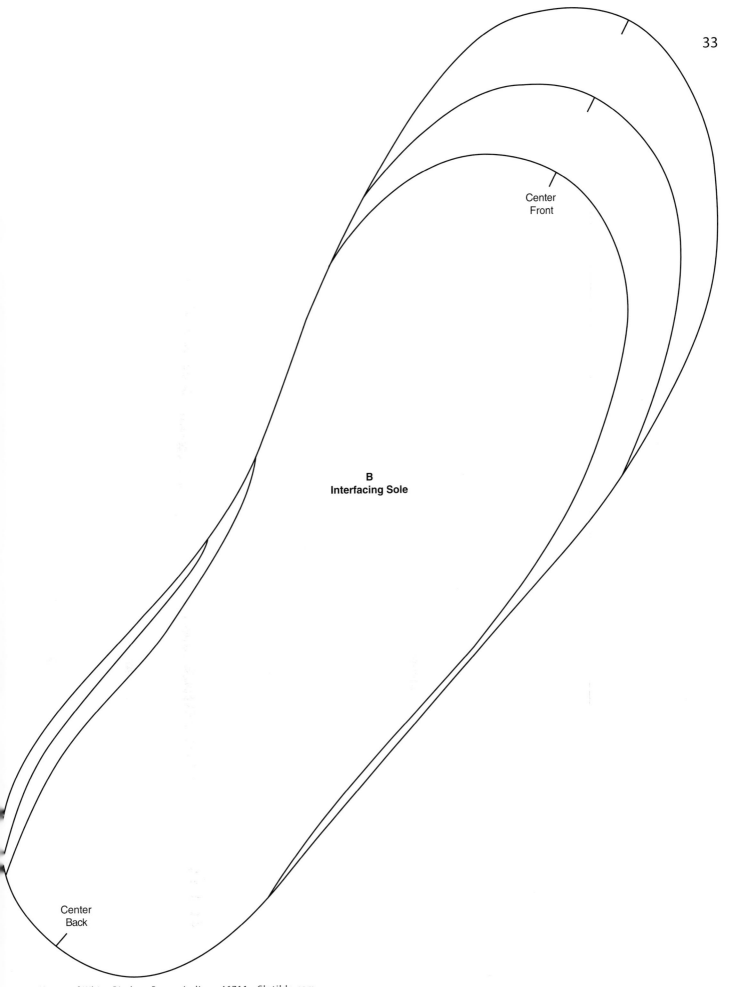

Center
Front

B
Interfacing Sole

Center
Back

House of White Birches, Berne, Indiana 46711   Clotilde.com

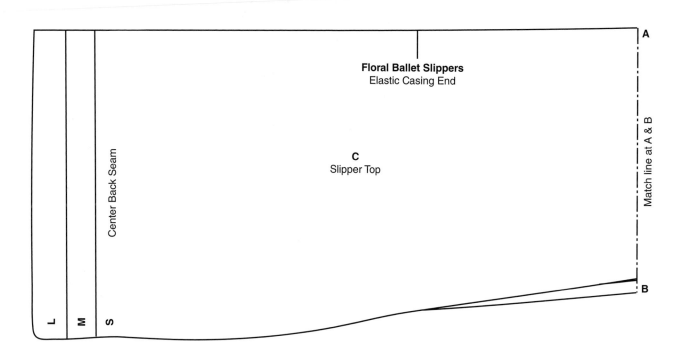

Floral Ballet Slippers
Elastic Casing End

C
Slipper Top

Center Back Seam

Match line at A & B

A

B

L M S

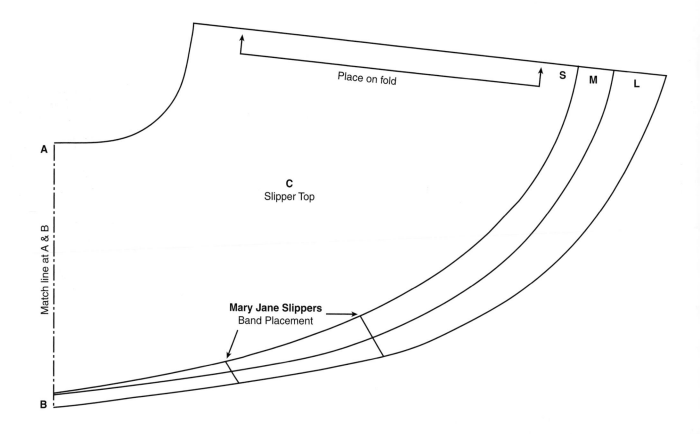

Place on fold

C
Slipper Top

Match line at A & B

A

B

S M L

Mary Jane Slippers
Band Placement

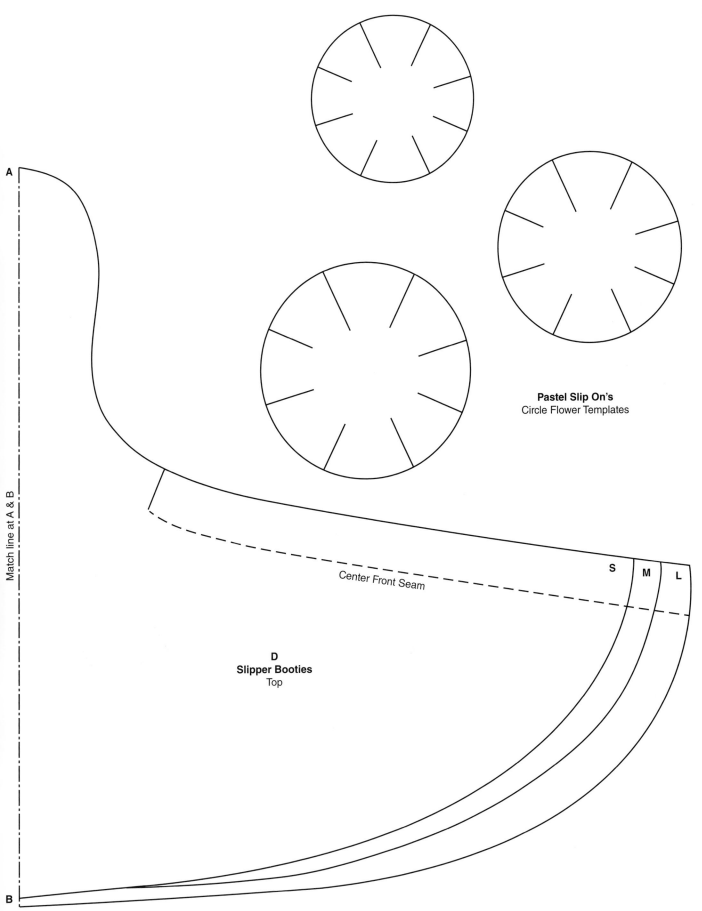

Pastel Slip On's
Circle Flower Templates

A

Match line at A & B

Center Front Seam

S M L

D
Slipper Booties
Top

B

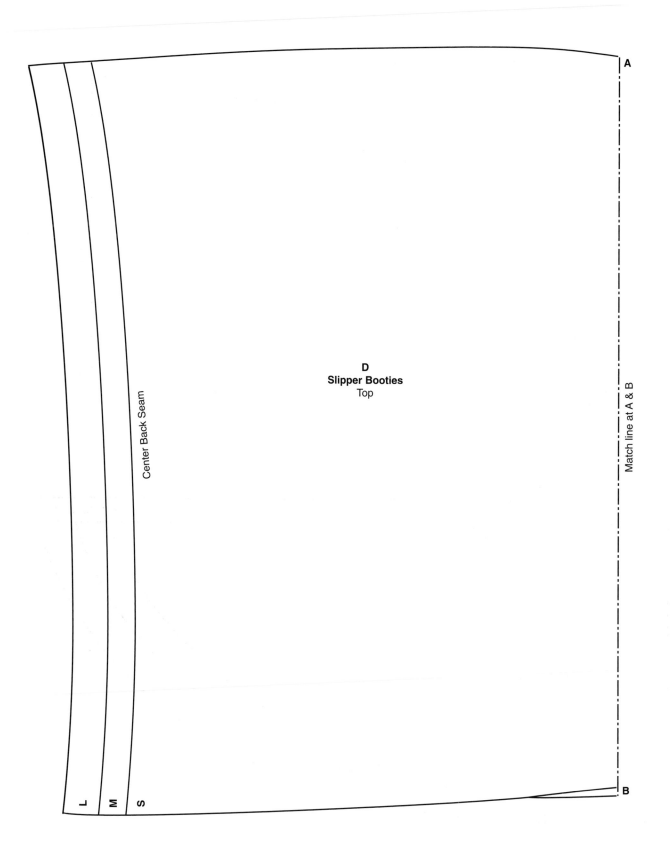

A

B

Match line at A & B

Center Back Seam

D
Slipper Booties
Top

L M S

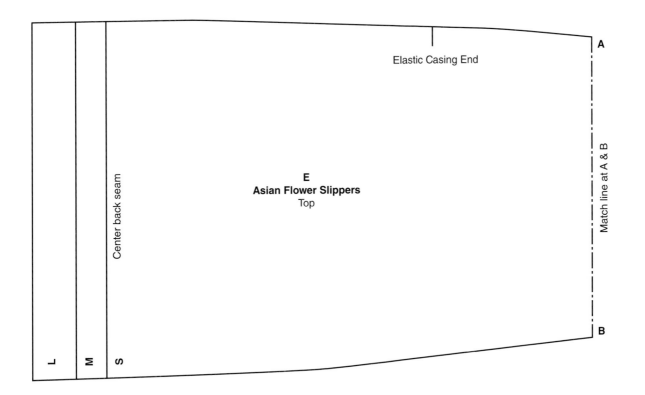

Elastic Casing End

E
Asian Flower Slippers
Top

Center back seam

Match line at A & B

A

B

L M S

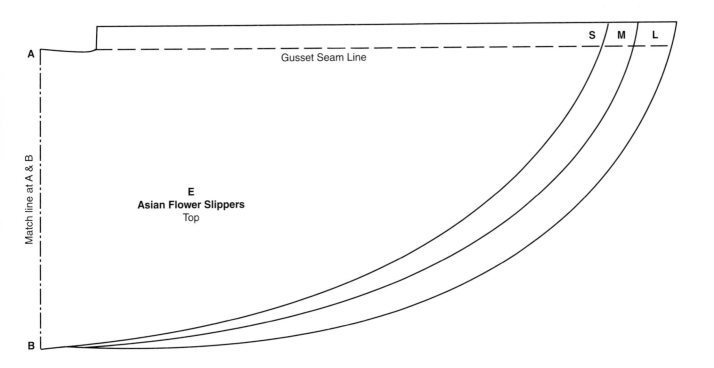

Gusset Seam Line

S M L

A

B

Match line at A & B

E
Asian Flower Slippers
Top

House of White Birches, Berne, Indiana 46711   Clotilde.com

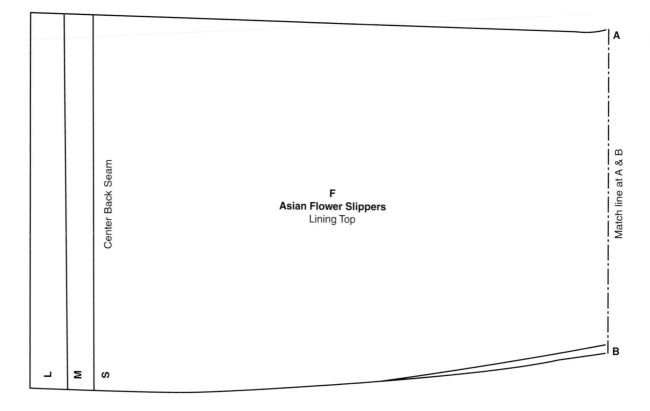

Center Back Seam

Match line at A & B

F
Asian Flower Slippers
Lining Top

L M S

A

B

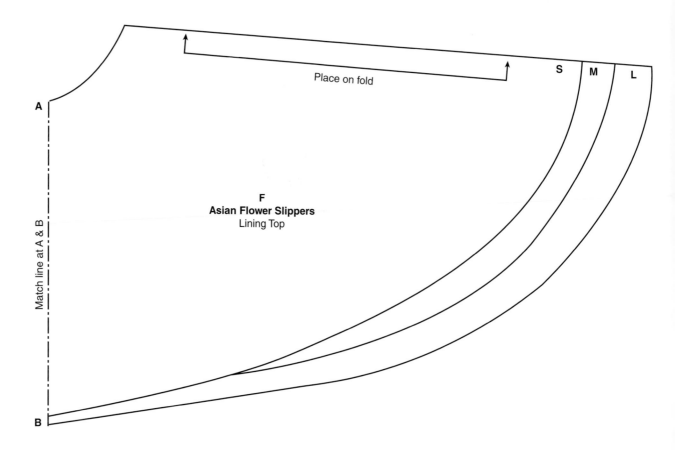

Place on fold

S M L

Match line at A & B

F
Asian Flower Slippers
Lining Top

A

B

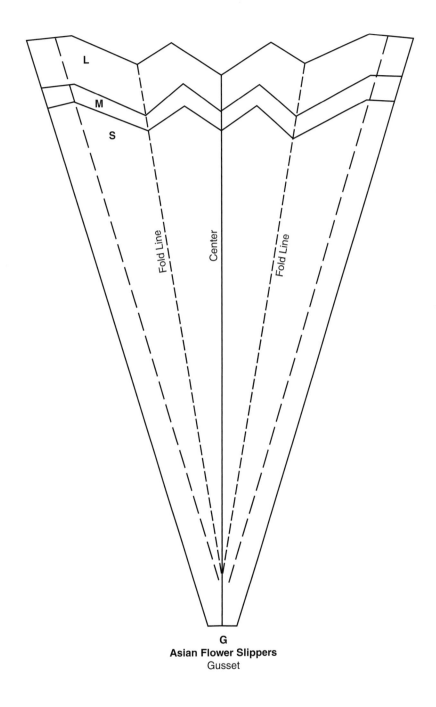

L

M

S

Fold Line

Center

Fold Line

G
Asian Flower Slippers
Gusset

House of White Birches, Berne, Indiana 46711   Clotilde.com

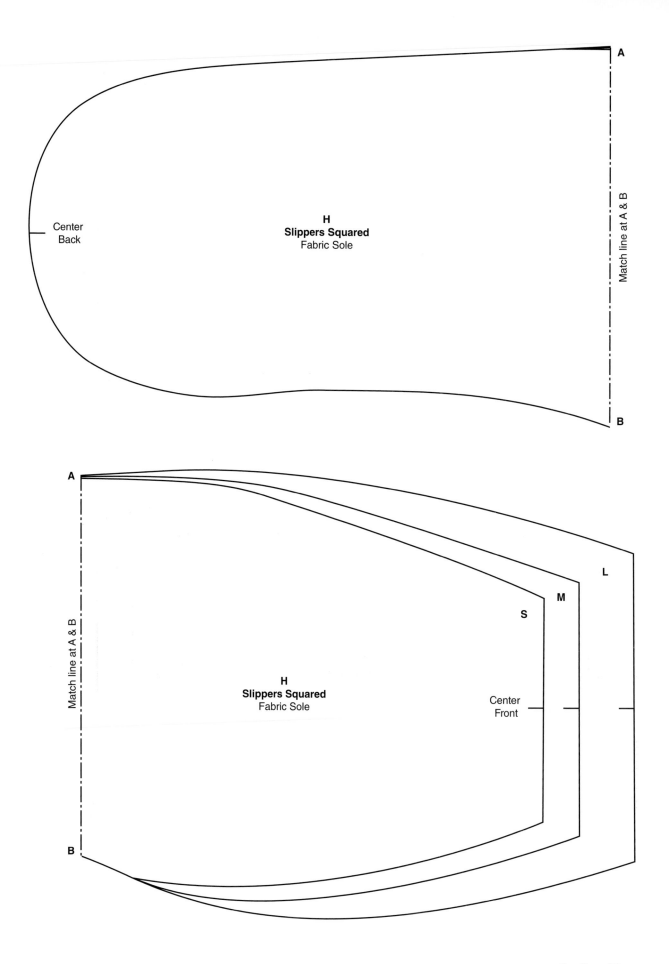

Center
Back

H
Slippers Squared
Fabric Sole

Match line at A & B

A

B

A

Match line at A & B

B

S

M

L

H
Slippers Squared
Fabric Sole

Center
Front

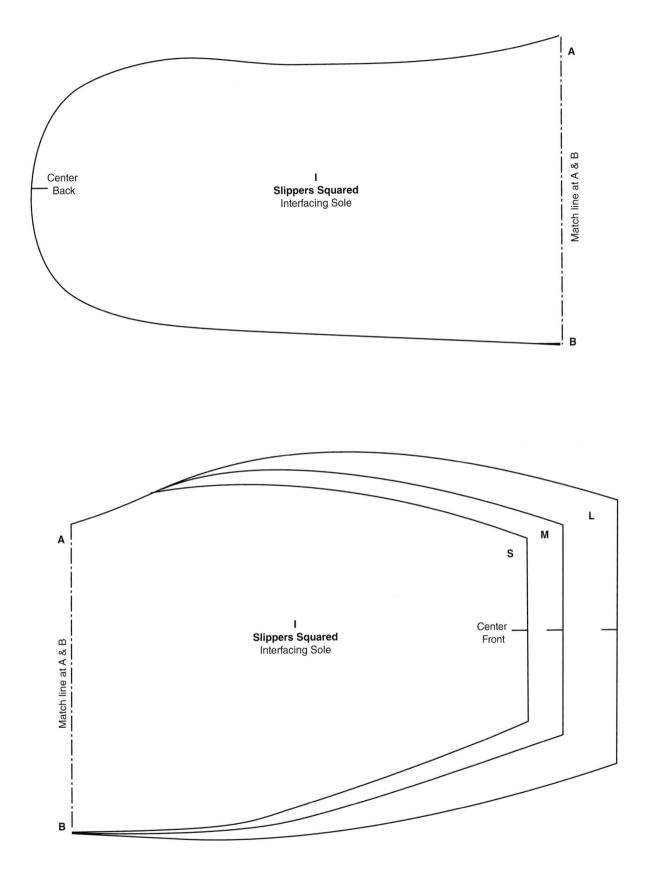

Center Back

I
Slippers Squared
Interfacing Sole

Match line at A & B

A

B

A

I
Slippers Squared
Interfacing Sole

Match line at A & B

B

S

M

L

Center Front

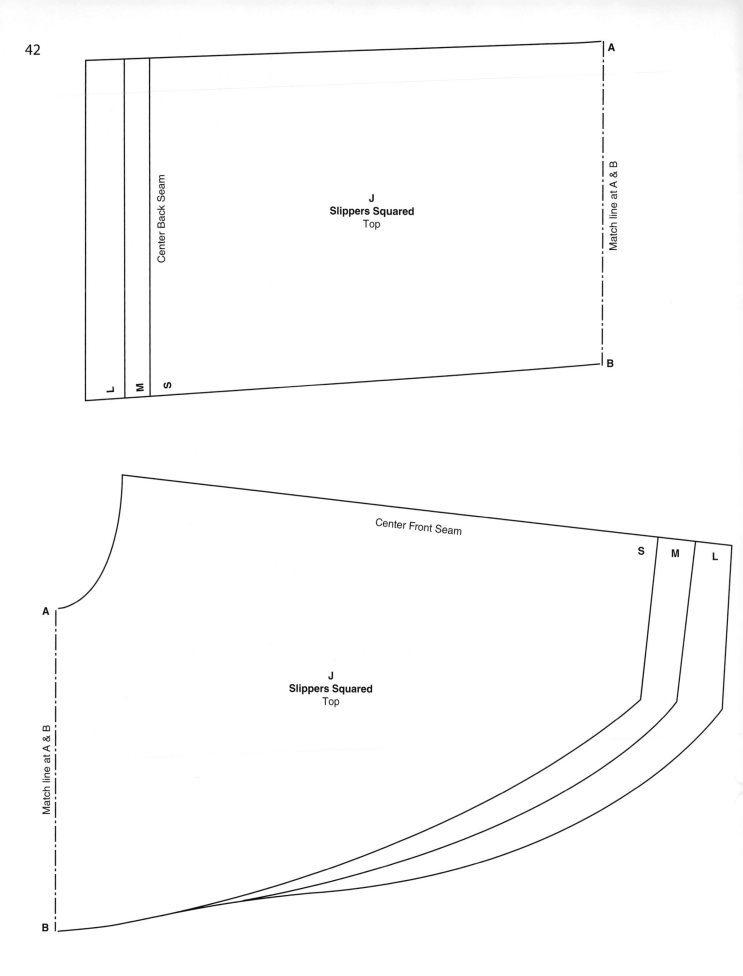

A

Match line at A & B

Center Back Seam

L M S

J
Slippers Squared
Top

B

Center Front Seam

S M L

A

Match line at A & B

J
Slippers Squared
Top

B

Slipper Booties
Flower Templates

K
Slippers Squared
Bow

44

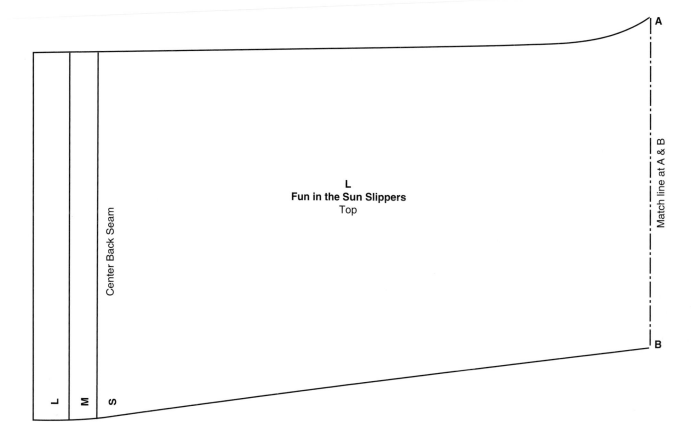

L
Fun in the Sun Slippers
Top

Center Back Seam

Match line at A & B

A

B

L M S

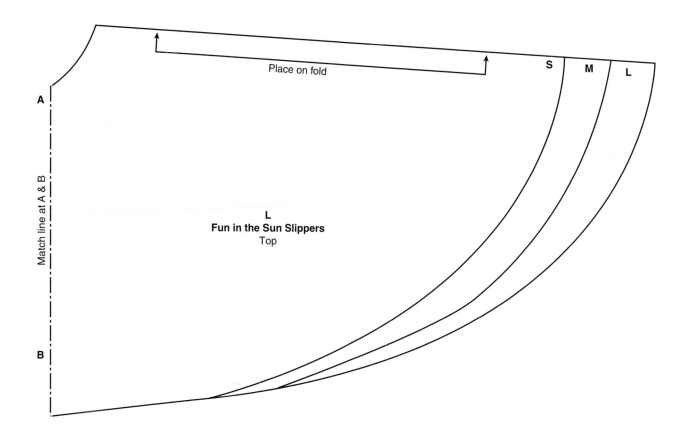

Match line at A & B

A

B

Place on fold

S M L

L
Fun in the Sun Slippers
Top

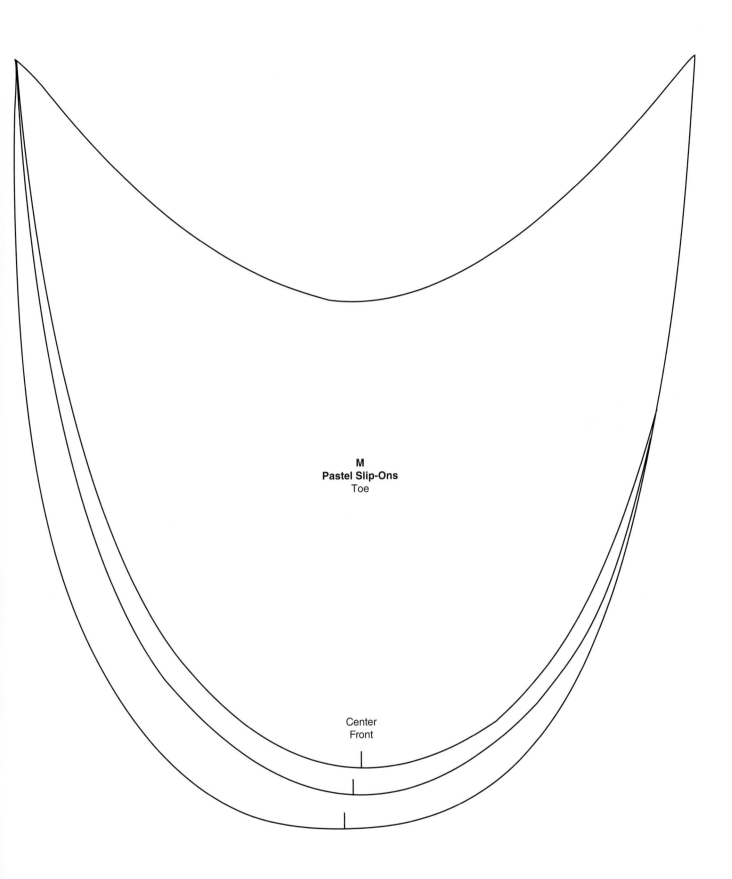

M
Pastel Slip-Ons
Toe

Center
Front

House of White Birches, Berne, Indiana 46711   Clotilde.com

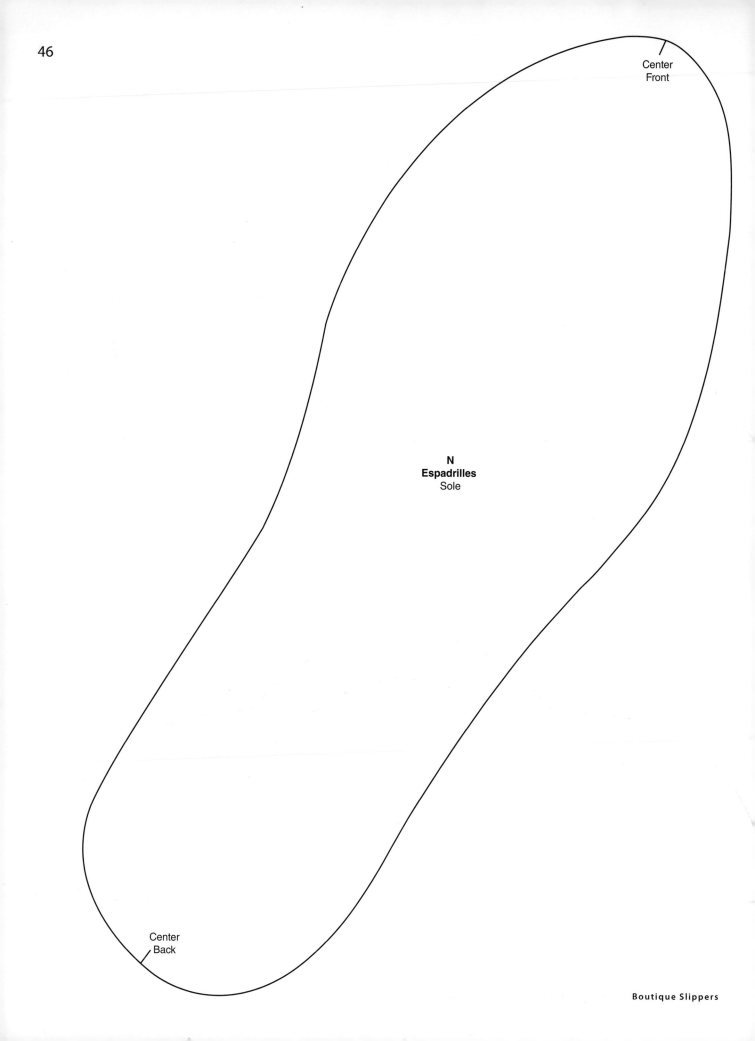

Center
Front

N
Espadrilles
Sole

Center
Back

Boutique Slippers

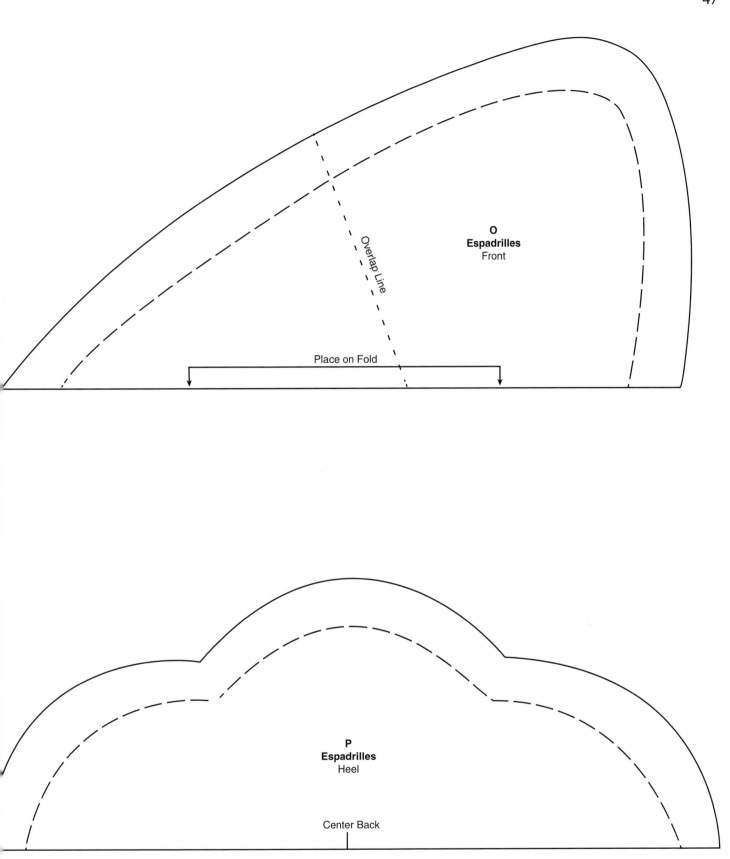

O
Espadrilles
Front

Overlap Line

Place on Fold

P
Espadrilles
Heel

Center Back

House of White Birches, Berne, Indiana 46711   Clotilde.com

Photo Index

Boutique Slippers is published by DRG, 306 East Parr Road, Berne, IN 46711. Printed in USA. Copyright © 2011 DRG. All rights reserved. This publication may not be reproduced in part or in whole without written permission from the publisher.

RETAIL STORES: If you would like to carry this pattern book or any other DRG publications, visit DRGwholesale.com

Every effort has been made to ensure that the instructions in this pattern book are complete and accurate. We cannot, however, take responsibility for human error, typographical mistakes or variations in individual work. Please visit ClotildeCustomerCare.com to check for pattern updates.

HOUSE of
WHITE
BIRCHES
PUBLISHERS
SINCE 1947

ISBN: 978-1-59217-340-2

23456789